ANIMAL ABILITIES

RATS

Anna Claybourne

Raintree is an imprint of Capstone Global Library Limited, a company incorporated in England and Wales having its registered office at 7 Pilgrim Street, London, EC4V 6LB – Registered company number: 6695582

To contact Raintree, please phone 0845 6044371, fax +44 (0) 1865 312263, or email myorders@ raintreepublishers.co.uk.

Text © Capstone Global Library Limited 2013
First published in hardback in 2013
The moral rights of the proprietor have been asserted.

Edited by Laura Knowles, Abby Colich,
    and Diyan Leake
Designed by Victoria Allen
Original illustrations © Capstone Global
    Library Ltd 2013
Illustrated by HL Studios
Picture research by Elizabeth Alexander
Originated by Capstone Global Library Ltd
Printed and bound in China by CTPS

ISBN 978 1 406 25913 1
17 16 15 14 13
10 9 8 7 6 5 4 3 2 1

British Library Cataloguing in Publication Data
Claybourne, Anna.
    Rats. -- (Animal abilities)
    1. Rats--Juvenile literature. 2. Animal intelligence--
    Juvenile literature.
    I. Title II. Series
    599.3'5-dc23

Acknowledgements

We would like to thank the following for permission to reproduce photographs: Alamy pp. 7 (© Visual&Written SL), 12 (© Juniors Bildarchiv GmbH), 19 (© Mary Evans Picture Library); Corbis pp. 20 (© Bettmann), 21 (© Elke Van De Velde), 22 (© Wolfgang Flamisch), 25 (© Emmanuel Kwitema/Reuters), 29 left (© Michael Durham/Minden Pictures); FLPA p. 18 (© Erica Olsen); Getty Images pp. 24 (Yasuyoshi Chiba/AFP), 26 (Pierre Verdy/AFP); Nature Picture Library pp. 4 (© Warwick Sloss), 6 (© Gary K. Smith), 13 (© Steimer/ARCO); Newscom p. 16 (Splash News); Photoshot pp. 5 (NHPA/Daniel Heuclin), 10 (BSIP); public domain/ Joseph Smit p. 28; Science Photo Library pp. 11 (Patrick Landmann), 27 (George Steinmetz); Shutterstock pp. 8 (© Volkova), 9 (© Artmim), 14 (© constructer), 15 (© Oshchepkov Dmitry), 29 right (© Elena Larina). Design feature of a rat silhoutte reproduced courtesy of Shutterstock (© Potapov Alexander).

Cover photograph of a rat reproduced with permission of Shutterstock (© Pakhnyushch).

Every effort has been made to contact copyright holders of material reproduced in this book. Any omissions will be rectified in subsequent printings if notice is given to the publisher.

Disclaimer

Contents

Some words are shown in bold, **like this**. You can find out what they mean by looking in the glossary.

Meet the rat

Rats are everywhere! These small, furry **rodents** live almost anywhere humans live, as well as in the wild. Rats are tough and clever, and can survive on almost any food. This is how they've managed to spread all over the world.

Common rats

When you think of a rat, it's probably a brown rat or black rat. These are the two most common **species** (types) in towns and cities. Black rats are usually smaller and darker than brown rats, and have longer tails. A brown rat can be 50 centimetres (20 inches) long from nose to tail – the length of a small dog!

This brown rat is sniffing around a dustbin by night.

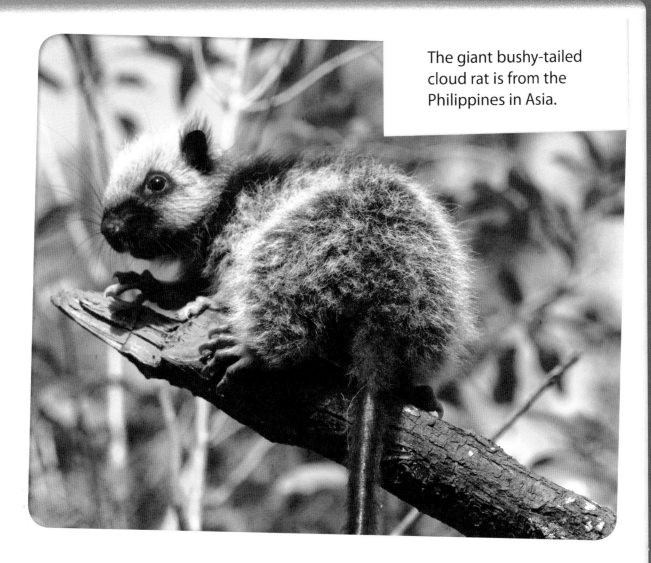

The giant bushy-tailed cloud rat is from the Philippines in Asia.

The rat family

There are many other kinds of rat, such as the rare and strangely named nonsense rat from India! The African giant pouched rat is one of the biggest of all, reaching nearly a metre (40 inches) long, including its tail.

RAT NICKNAMES

Rats have a lot of nicknames —
Brown rat: *common rat, street rat, sewer rat, Norway rat*
Black rat: *roof rat, ship rat, house rat, Old English rat*

Being a rat

Most rats are **nocturnal** and come out at night to look for food. During the day, they hide away in their dens, burrows, or nests.

Brown rats are good at swimming, and often live in sewers.

Where is home?

In the countryside, rats may make burrows or nest in trees. In towns, they live in lots of places, such as under sheds, in attics, or in farm buildings. They can also live in gardens, underground stations, and rubbish dumps.

Lots of rats!

Rats are social animals which live in groups. If they have enough food, there can be hundreds of rats living together. Each rat only lives for around 1–2 years, but rats have a *lot* of babies, so their numbers can grow fast. A female rat gives birth up to 10 times a year, with around eight babies (called pups or kittens) in each litter.

ARE RATS ENDANGERED?

A few types of rats are **endangered**, such as the nonsense rat, which only lives on a few islands in India. But black and brown rats are so common that in some places they can threaten other species.

This is a mother brown rat with a litter of pups.

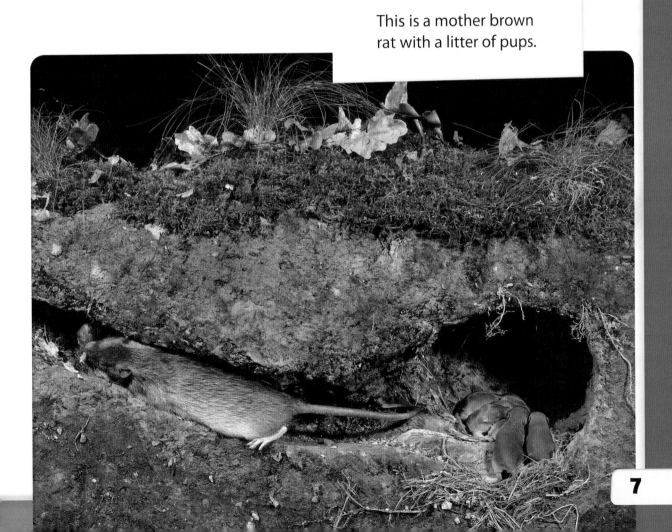

Rat bodies

Rats are **mammals**. They are warm-blooded, covered in hair, and feed their babies on milk.

In this picture of a brown rat, you can see the main parts of a typical rat's body.

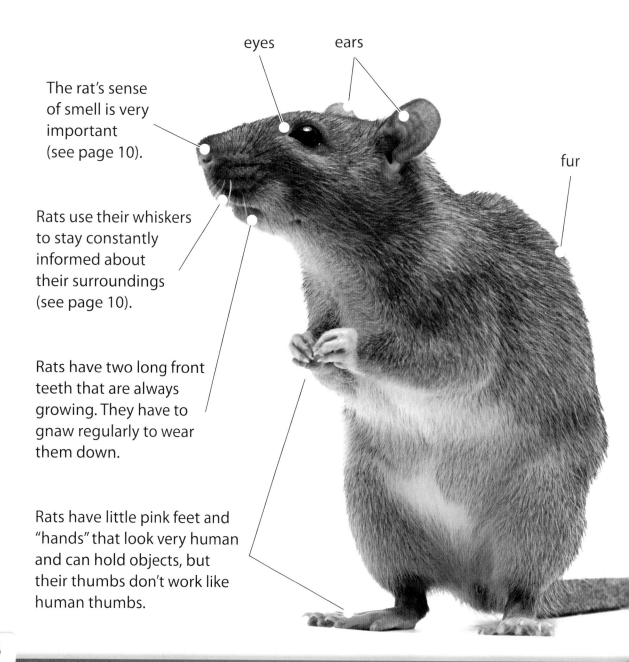

eyes

ears

fur

The rat's sense of smell is very important (see page 10).

Rats use their whiskers to stay constantly informed about their surroundings (see page 10).

Rats have two long front teeth that are always growing. They have to gnaw regularly to wear them down.

Rats have little pink feet and "hands" that look very human and can hold objects, but their thumbs don't work like human thumbs.

A TIGHT SQUEEZE

A medium-sized rat can wriggle through a gap the width of a 50 pence piece. This is why it can be hard to keep rats out of houses — they can squeeze under doors, between floorboards, or through other small gaps.

A rat's tail has no fur on it. It's used for controlling body temperature and balance. A few types of rat can also use their tails to hold onto things.

Rats often use their hands to hold on to food as they eat it.

Rat brains and senses

Rats are not the cleverest of animals, but they do well on intelligence tests set for them by scientists. They have some pretty amazing sensing abilities, too.

Sensing the world

Rats can't see very well, but they have a brilliant sense of smell, which they use to find food, sniff out danger, and recognize other rats. They also have very sharp hearing. They can detect quieter and higher sounds than humans can, so they can hear each other's high-pitched squeaks.

A rat's whiskers are super-sensitive. They can detect different textures and surfaces, and even pick up sound waves from the air. Rats often run around in dark narrow spaces such as burrows, so they use their whiskers to feel everything around them as they go.

A rat's whiskers brush against everything it runs past, and send signals to its brain.

Rats can find their way around mazes because of their good memory for the spaces around them and their sense of direction.

HOW DO WE KNOW?

One rat intelligence test found that if rats think they can't solve a puzzle with a big reward, they will choose not to take the test, and opt for a small reward instead. This means rats have a skill that's unusual for animals — they can think about their own knowledge and abilities, the way humans can.

Rat packs

Rats usually live in small groups, called **packs** or clans. A pack can be all male, all female, or a mixture. Rats rely on their pack, and being close to other rats is very important to them. They often snuggle up together, and **groom** and wash each other.

A pack of rats cuddle up together to sleep.

Who's in the pack?

Female packs contain a handful of mothers and their babies. They share a nest and help each other care for their pups. Meanwhile, male rats roam around in their own groups, or sometimes join with females to make a mixed pack.

No, I'm the boss!

Every rat has its own role in the pack. Rats chase, nip, groom, and play-fight to remind each other of everyone's position. For example, a **dominant** rat can pin another rat down and stand over it, to show he's in charge.

Pet rats will play the way that rats do in the wild.

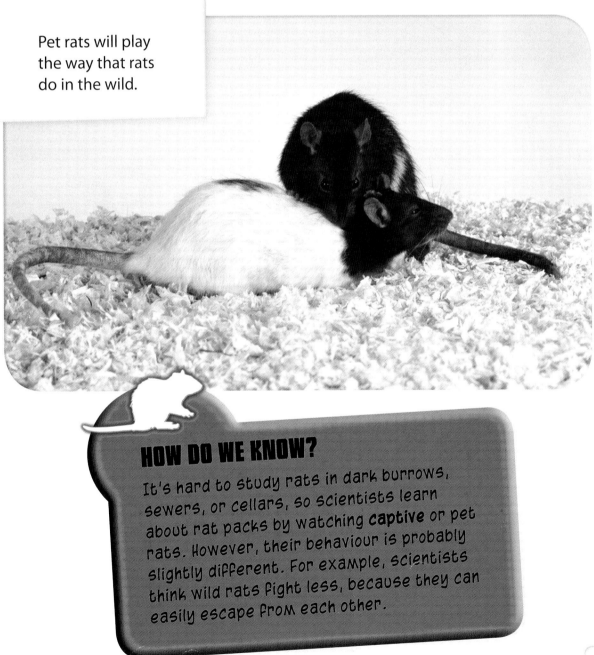

HOW DO WE KNOW?

It's hard to study rats in dark burrows, sewers, or cellars, so scientists learn about rat packs by watching **captive** or pet rats. However, their behaviour is probably slightly different. For example, scientists think wild rats fight less, because they can easily escape from each other.

Rat chat

Rats "talk" to each other all the time. They do this in two main ways: smell and sound.

Sniff... sniff...

Rats can easily tell their pack members from other rats by their smell. Also, each rat leaves a trail of urine (wee) wherever it goes. It contains smelly chemicals called **pheromones** that tell other rats whether it is male or female, its age, and even its role in its pack. Rats have a special second nose for detecting pheromones. It's called the vomeronasal organ, or VNO, and is found in a tiny passageway, just inside the rat's main nose.

A rat sniffs along the ground to read urine markings.

HOW DO WE KNOW?

To study rat pheromones, scientists can keep rats in separate enclosures and expose them to different smells from other rats, one at a time. Then they watch how this affects their behaviour.

Squeeeeak!

Just like in cartoons, rats really do squeak. In fact, they make all kinds of sounds, including chattering, chirping, and hissing. Many are **ultrasonic** – too high pitched for humans to hear. Some scientists say rats even seem to laugh when they're tickled!

SPEAK RAT

Sound	Meaning
Loud teeth chattering	I'm feeling anxious
Loud shriek	Ouch!
Long squeak	I don't like this, stop it!
"Bruxing", or gently grinding teeth	Ahh, I'm relaxed and content
Hissing	Don't mess with me!
Short squeak	I'm play-fighting!
Bwip!	I'm being groomed by another rat!

Rats sniff and squeak to get information about the world around them.

Learning

All animals have some abilities they don't have to learn, such as swallowing food or blinking. These abilities are called instincts. But some animals, such as rats, are also very good at learning new things.

Pet rats can learn to do tricks.

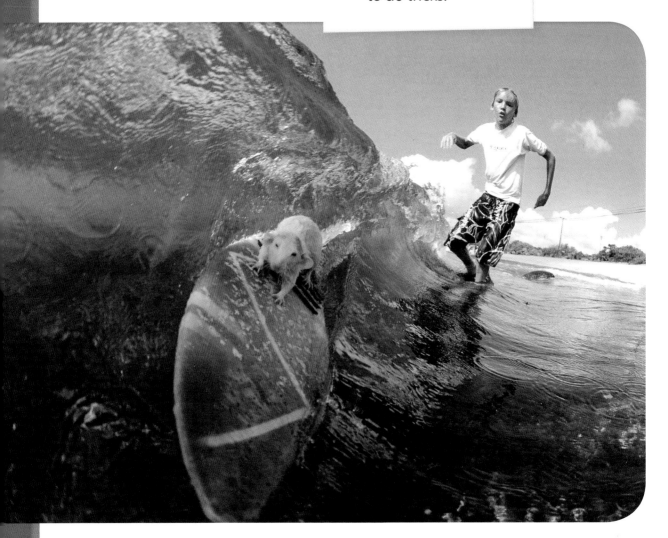

Growing up

Baby rats learn their own mother's smell, so they can tell her apart from other rats. They also learn which foods are safe to eat, and the pattern of pathways around their nest.

HOW DO WE KNOW?

Scientists began making mazes for rats around the year 1900. One early experimenter, Willard Small, built a model of the human-sized maze at Hampton Court Palace in London. He found that rats could solve it quite easily, and quickly became better and better at doing so.

In lab tests, rats can find their way through a maze, learn the route, and remember it. They may have developed this skill because they have to remember where all their pathways or burrows are in the wild.

Wild rat burrow system

Small's Hampton Court rat maze

Adapting

Adapting means changing to suit the situation you're in. Rats are brilliant at this, especially brown rats. They can easily switch between different homes, foods, and climates. This is one reason why rats are so good at surviving.

Ratty room-mates

Rats have existed for much longer than humans. But when humans first appeared, and began building homes, growing crops, and using fires to cook and keep warm, it gave rats a free ride. Many rats adapted to living with humans, so they could use our warm homes, food stores, and tasty leftovers.

This brown rat is helping itself to a takeaway meal.

Rats on a journey

As humans spread around the world, rats went with them, hitching a ride on boats and grain wagons. Rats coped easily with the new foods and surroundings. Many other animals, such as pandas, could not do this, as they are suited to only one particular place or lifestyle.

This old illustration shows rats making their way ashore along a ship's ropes.

RAT FOOD

Rats will eat almost any food, including:
- fruit and vegetables
- plants
- meat
- nuts and seeds
- chocolate
- frogs
- small mammals
- insects
- bones
- any human rubbish or leftovers
- carrion (dead animals)
- vomit...
- ...and even animal poo!

Pests or pets?

As far as humans are concerned, rats are both pests and pets! When they live alongside us, rats can make a terrible mess. They chew wood, paper, and electrical wires to make their nests and to keep their teeth short. And they wee and poo everywhere!

This is a scene from the days of the Black Death, when carts collected dead bodies in the streets.

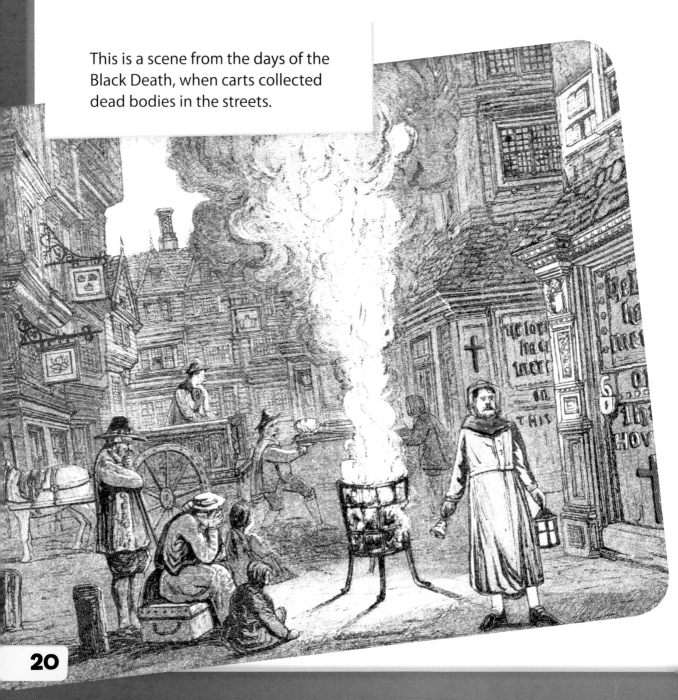

Deadly diseases

One reason why you shouldn't touch wild rats is that they can carry dangerous diseases. The worst example ever was the bubonic plague, or Black Death. Rats caught the disease, then fleas spread the plague germs from rats to humans in their bites. In the 1300s, the plague spread across Europe, killing 25 million people.

HOW DO WE KNOW?

Scientists did not discover what caused the plague or how it spread until the 1890s, when the latest microscopes allowed them to learn much more about germs and how they work.

Pet rats

Rats can be great pets, because they are so clever and sociable. Like dogs, they get very attached to their owners. Pet rats were first bred from brown rats, but now come in many varieties and colours. Some are even bald!

Pet rats usually live in cages, but some owners carry them around with them.

Lab rats

Rats have been used in lab experiments for almost 200 years, to study germs and diseases, intelligence, and much more. As they are similar to us in some ways, they are also used to test medicines.

Meet the lab rat

Lab rats were bred from brown rats, but they now look very different. They are mainly white, and there are several different types or **strains**:

- Wistar rat – lab rat that is an albino (has little or no natural colour), for general use

- Sprague Dawley rat – white, calm, easy-going rat

- Zucker rat – a very hungry, fat rat, used to study **obesity**

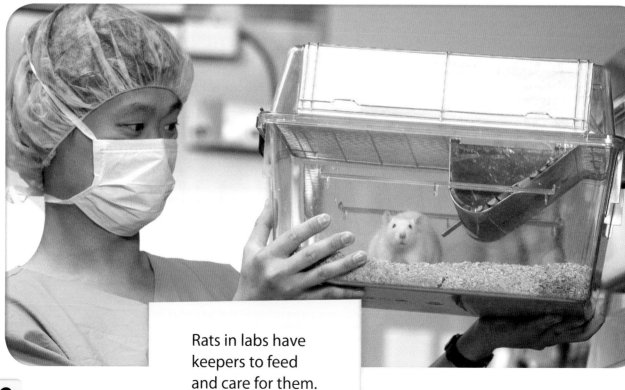

Rats in labs have keepers to feed and care for them.

IS IT CRUEL?

Some people say using any animal in science labs is cruel and wrong. Others say it's OK if the rats are treated well. Some rat experiments, such as medical tests, save human lives. Lab rats are specially bred, and wouldn't have a life at all otherwise — though it's not a natural life. What do you think?

First attempt

Underwater platform

Start

Water has been whitened so rat cannot see platform

Eighth attempt

Underwater platform

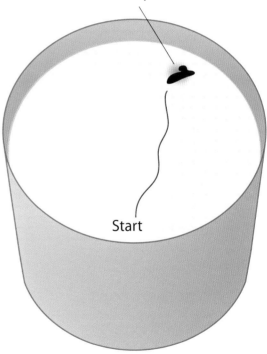

Start

At first, rats take a while to find the platform. But over several tries, they learn where it is.

The Morris water maze experiment is often used to test rats' abilities. It's perfectly suited to brown rats, because they are good swimmers.

Working with rats

Rats' amazing abilities mean they can sometimes do things humans can't. Like dogs, rats can combine their brilliant sense of smell with their learning abilities, and learn to detect particular scents. Some rats help doctors by spotting the smell of diseases such as **tuberculosis**. In war zones in Africa, giant pouched rats have been trained to sniff out **landmines**, so that they can be safely removed.

A rat learns to detect the smell of tuberculosis by sniffing samples of spit taken from patients.

A tight squeeze

One rat (called Rattie) in California, USA, has even been trained to help wire up school computer networks, by pulling a string along inside walls and ceilings to guide the cables into place. Rats' ability to get through narrow gaps could be used for other things, too, such as helping to find people trapped in mines, caves, or collapsed buildings.

This giant pouched rat is trained to sniff for landmines in Africa.

RAT STARS

Rats also work in entertainment. You might have seen them doing tricks in circus or street shows, and directors can book specially trained rats to perform in films or on television.

Copying rats

You might think of a robot as human-shaped, but more and more scientists are building robots inspired by animals. They include "ratbots", or rat robots.

Ratbots

Most ratbots focus on a special ratty feature humans don't have – their super-sensitive whiskers. Robots with thin, flexible, plastic whiskers can sense their surroundings, like a real rat. They could be used in hard-to-reach or dark places, to find earthquake survivors, for example.

In one experiment, real rat brain cells are being used to control robot rats. These ratbots are very simple at the moment, but they are revealing a lot about how brain cells learn and grow.

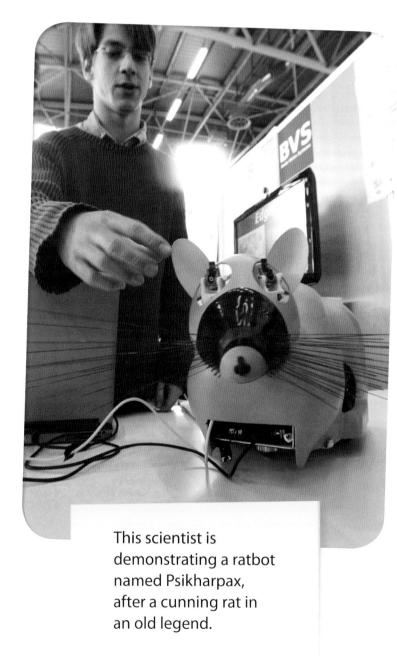

This scientist is demonstrating a ratbot named Psikharpax, after a cunning rat in an old legend.

Remote-controlled rats

Scientists have also created "remote-controlled" real live rats, by fitting electrical implants into their brains, and sending wireless signals from a laptop to control them. It sounds like something from a sci-fi film, but the rats don't seem to be upset by the experience. This work could pave the way for remote-control devices for humans, to do things such as help paralysed people to control their limbs.

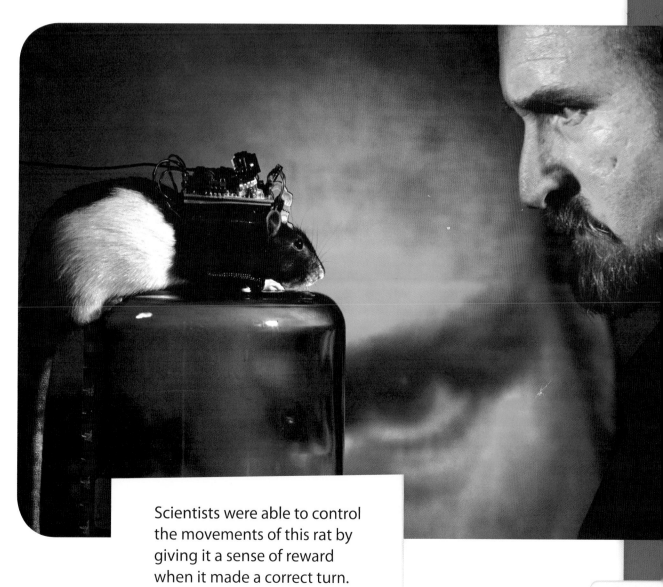

Scientists were able to control the movements of this rat by giving it a sense of reward when it made a correct turn.

The amazing rat

Many people are horrified by rats. For centuries, they've raided our food stores, nibbled holes in our walls, and spread diseases. Sometimes, we have to take measures to control rat populations, or else they would take over our homes! So rats and humans can certainly be enemies.

Rats like this one became **extinct** in 1903.

But maybe after reading this book, you'll see rats in a different light! We've only recently realized just how clever rats are. By working together with rats, at least some of the time, we can learn more about their amazing abilities.

Rat superpowers

If you could pick one of the rat's amazing superhuman abilities, which would you choose?

- If you had super-sensing whiskers like a rat's, you could easily feel your way in the dark, and you'd constantly be sensing the textures all around you. You'd look a bit strange, though!

- If you had ultrasonic hearing like a rat's, you could listen to sounds made by bats, rats, dolphins, and other ultrasonic animals, but you'd probably be annoyed by sounds from computers and gadgets that people can't normally hear.

- If you had scent signal detection like a rat's, you could find anything you'd lost by sniffing it out, and track down a snack easily.

- If you had an amazing ratty tail, you could balance as you ran along rooftops. Handy for escaping the crowds on the pavement!

Bats and dolphins have ultrasonic hearing like a rat's.

Glossary

captive   held in a zoo, aquarium, or laboratory instead of living in the wild

dominant   having the most power and control

endangered   at risk of dying out

extinct   has died out forever

groom   clean the fur or skin

landmine   small bomb designed to go off when someone steps on it

mammal   type of warm-blooded animal that has a backbone, feeds on its mother's milk when young, and has hair on its body

nocturnal   active at night

obesity   state of being very overweight

pack   group of rats that live together

pheromone   chemical released from an animal's body to send a message

rodent   type of small furry mammal. Rats, mice, squirrels, and hamsters are all rodents.

species   particular type of living thing

strains   types of animal within the same species, but with different features

tuberculosis   disease that can destroy the lungs or other body parts

ultrasonic   too high pitched for humans to hear naturally

Find out more

Books

Rat (Animal Neighbours), Stephen Savage (Wayland, 2007)

Rats (What's Awake?), Patricia Whitehouse (Raintree, 2009)

The Secret Life of Rats (Extreme Science), Trevor Day (A&C Black, 2009)

Websites

www.apopo.org/cms.php?cmsid=107
Discover all about the organization that trains giant pouched rats to sniff out landmines.

www.arkive.org/black-rat/rattus-rattus
www.arkive.org/brown-rat/rattus-norvegicus
Find out more about the brown rat (*Rattus norvegicus*) and the black rat (*Rattus rattus*) on Arkive's website.

www.bbc.co.uk/nature/life/Brown_rat
Useful brown rat facts, along with a selection of top-quality film clips, can be found on the BBC website.

www.bbc.co.uk/nature/life/Mallomys#p004hfq9
See the newly discovered Bosavi woolly rat on video!

www.nfrs.org/shortinfo.html
For expert advice, tips, and things to think about if you are considering a pet rat, have a look at the National Fancy Rat Society's website.

Places to visit

You can see black, brown, and other rats at many zoos, including:

Bristol Zoo Gardens
Clifton
Bristol BS8 3HA
www.bristolzoo.org.uk
Bristol Zoo has a rat and mouse exhibit built to look like a creaky old house.

Wingham Wildlife Park
Wingham
Canterbury
Kent CT3 1JL
www.winghamwildlifepark.co.uk

Index